D1382404

Gallery Books
Editor Peter Fallon

STAY

Andrew Jamison

STAY

Gallery Books

Stay
is first published
simultaneously in paperback
and in a clothbound edition
on 28 September 2017.

The Gallery Press
Loughcrew
Oldcastle
County Meath
Ireland

www.gallerypress.com

ISBN 978 1 91133 703 4 *paperback*
     978 1 91133 704 1 *clothbound*

A CIP catalogue record for this book
is available from the British Library.

Stay receives financial assistance
from the Arts Councils of Ireland.

Contents

for Aimée

The Reading

Early mornings, long mornings of low heart rate,
softened shoulders, strong supermarket tea,
the sofa. Days of pages and page silence.
Months mingled with traffic and talk from the street
through the opened window as you read.
As you read you notice the fig plant,
parts of it dying, parts of it flourishing
exponentially — you've read that word recently.
The reading is teaching you to leave such things
alone, to keep the TV off, forgo
the internet searches for property;
interest rates, share prices will still be in flux
when you return after reading. Reading
so long that the light has changed, that it's time
to put on the lamps so you can read some more
about the family trying to get work
in nineteenth-century California
as fruit pickers. Reading, remembering
you've forgotten to eat. Reading on and freed
from the millstone of your own ego — *phew.*
Reading when you're not reading: reading the sky
on a Sunday at half-seven in August
when someone you love is making you dinner
and you're late. Reading a kiss, reading a body
in the summer in the morning
before you start reading about the boys who've escaped
on horseback and are heading south, Mexico way.
Reading the next line before you've finished
the one you're on. Reading the last
line by accident and spoiling it for yourself.
Reading that bit all over again and again.
On a nudist beach in a foreign country,
reading, despite the fascinating array
of genitalia parading up
and down the tide line; reading instead

a scene in which a woman who has nothing,
not even her stillborn child, gives suck
to a septuagenarian who hasn't eaten
for so long he's skin and bone. Indoors,
reading, on the hottest day of the year, trying
to read all the reading you can humanly read
in the life you have left to read it in.

Words for Summer

I've wondered if there are words for it,
the end of August, all this loving you.
Blackberries at Burrington, the sea at Brean,
a half of something local at The Plough,
in its garden in the sun in the heat,
or trying to learn to dance, where to stand,
how not to grip your hands too tightly in the hold,
the right amount of tension in the arms.

I've wondered if there will be words for it
again, now summer's over, and life,
the working world, with timetables and terms,
is calling our names in its register
to which we must respond with 'here' or 'present'
even if we're not, thinking only
of garden and picked fruit, The Plough and the sea,
of hands and of arms and of holding.

The Night You Became a County

Not even a week away and it's been tough
to see a thing as a thing in itself
without seeing something of you. Take the Mournes
visible from a Killyleagh hill,
how their undulations took on your skin and bones,
each Slieve contouring into the next, anatomical;
your shoulder seemed so much like Donard,
your neck The Devil's Bite, your elbow Binnian.
And what was the water, Strangford Lough itself,
but your language, your words, your speaking voice,
not your whistling or your song — too good —
but your plain speech, telling me things:
words I wanted to hear, and words that were true.
Your accent went forgotten
until there was sight of the shoreline drawing
away to the north; and your breath, your breath,
your breath was the water of where I'm from.

Stay

I do not come from here, bay windows, Bath stone,
Georgian terraces, and I wish I had the words

like others to pin down this unbelonging
spindrift soul in me, unsettled,

always only half here. The sea at Sand Bay
washes up nothing but questions,

tired of themselves, like the question
of returning, to which the same answer returns.

The Party

after Chekhov

I can see you in the sunlight, Olga,
Olga Mikhaylovna, Olga Mikhaylovna,
a name that glimmers with its own sense of summer,
you are under the cherry trees and the plum trees,
uncomfortable in your corset, tugging at it;
you do not need to tell me that you're pregnant.
I know. The scent of hay and honey
and the brief buzz of bees; I am there beside you,
beside the wattle fence and the meadows,
fiddles and tambourines on the evening air.
I am walking with you through the hazel bushes,
over the raspberry patch and the croquet lawn
and you're telling me how uncertain you are.
You say 'osier' and I ask you what it means
but you don't give a definition.
I want, Olga, to pen a song for you,
call it 'Love Song for Olga Mikhaylovna'
but you couldn't be less interested if you tried.
I ask why you've escaped from your own party,
why I have found you walking all alone,
but even if you knew you wouldn't tell me.
And when you mention when you moved to town
for the first time, and you were bored stupid
so went to court hearings because Peter,
your husband, was busy, I don't know what to say.

Olga, Olga Mikhaylovna,
you've shown me the apple and the pear trees,
let me undo the laces at your back.
Put down the scythe. And stop eavesdropping
on young girls from the university.
Let's face the music, go back to the ballroom,
drink tea and converse on the veranda,

listen to piano from the drawing room,
drunken shouts, and strains of concertina.
Everyone will be wondering where we've been.

Stronghold

The weekend shouldn't feel like an island
but it does, between the weekday waters

of wanting you, which shouldn't feel like waters
but do, because of work and bills, careers

and the sea of having, in which we're adrift
from this fascination to own, to buy.

I hold you because there is so much of you,
dainty as you are, I cannot and will not hold.

Colmcille

after the Irish (anonymous, 6th century)

To go back to that place, that island,
to the North coast cliff tops, and
to catch the whisper of the sea with the sand.

To take in the waves unburdening
themselves of the glistering ocean, sounding
like something holy, unending.

To stand there, on the strand, not sad
about driftwood and shells and how they're clad
in light; the seagull's scrake; the horizon's charade.

To this day I can make out that soundscape
of Irish Sea on rock. I'll never escape
its eerie shoreline murmurings; make no mistake.

But to go back, to be there
for the sight of seabirds lifting together,
the one-off whale surfacing for air,

the tide coming in — a flood of foam —
and tell them who I really am,
'the one who turned his back on this, his home'.

Water

I've passed a glass to you in the aftermath
of night, to douse your lips, your throat, your mouth,

to slake your tongue, making it taste like new;
water is the word I want to say to you,

the word I want for you to hear me say
in the driest part of your burnt-out day,

'water', as if words could wash us
away from time, and how it parches.

The Line

I draw the line at seven o'clock;
I draw the line at evening, Strangford Lough

where I think of drawing the line at you
who draws the line, unswervingly, straight through

the bullshit in this 9-5 existence.
I'm drawing the line at the Mournes in the distance

reminding me to draw the line at fame,
money, to seek only the little acclaim

of the line itself, which draws a line at me,
who cannot draw a line at the Irish Sea.

What You Missed While Walking in the Wye Valley

Me, miming the high notes of 'The Sidewinder Sleeps Tonite'
in the kitchen, while stirring baked beans

which had been in the fridge for over a week —
'baby, instant soup doesn't really grab me' —

while toasting multi-seeded wholemeal bread —
'today I need something more sub-sub-sub-substantial.'

Me, staring out the window blearily,
open mouthed, at the trees and train tracks and sky

'like a heartbeat, baby, trying to wake up'
as if the words I wanted for you were dozing, there.

Souvenir

1

Close your eyes and you're on rue Saint-Jacques.
The rain has stopped and you're looking through

the window of the bakery. Can't you see
the families of *mille feuille* and *macarons*?

Say you can't feel the nectarines, peaches,
tomatoes on the vine in your hand,

can't hear the waspish buzz of *motos*
running lights. Can't you taste this bread

in its red and yellow paper bag,
the *petit cornet* of fries twice cooked in beef fat?

The smell of foreign money is on your hands;
there's a sleeping bag beggar against the wall,

he's saying to you '*bonjour, monsieur, bonjour*'.

2

Now you're on a rented bike, freewheeling
downhill, a cobbled passageway, catching

your reflection in the shopfronts that you pass.
Yes; that's you. Yes; you are here. Yes,

at the red light by the roundabout
at the end of rue Soufflot. There's no doubt

you see the Eiffel Tower above the trees
of the Luxembourg. The rain specked breeze

is pocking your shirt, your jeans, dampening
even more your shower-damp hair, mingling

with your sweat-pocked brow and clean-shaved top lip
which tastes of breakfast's strawberry jam as you slip —

it's morning, you're late — up or down into whatever gear
makes you quicker. You are getting nearer.

3

Close your eyes and you're cycling, sweating,
at night in a quarter you don't know, getting

farther away with every turn. Cafés are heaving
carafes, small tables, salads, laughter. You're weaving

side to side, head down, as you tire, uphill.
Now you're on track. Boulevard Saint-Michel.

You stop. Your linen shirt is stuck to your back.
You park. *Keep them closed.* The night is bright black.

4

You're in your room. The window is open.
You're on your bed. You have awoken.

It's just you and this Parisian summer sky;
its blue encounters the blue of your eye.

Someone is walking across the gravel
of the courtyard below. Unravel,

memory, that time, that city again,
its rue Mouffetard, its Gare de Lyon, its Seine.

5

Close your eyes and you're leaving. Morning.
Saturday. Grey. A waiter tautens an awning.

You're sprayed in the wake of the street-sweeping truck
on your way to the Métro. Your suitcase gets stuck

momentarily at the ticket barrier.
Now you're on the platform for the RER.

That feeling that you've left something behind.
That feeling that you've left something behind.

Remember That Night?

after the Irish (anonymous, 17th/18th century?)

Remember that night you came to the window
in neither coat nor gloves, barely a stitch on you?
I held out my hand and you grabbed it, no 'hello',
and we hung around till the nightingale was due.

Remember that night, that night when you and I
got a foundering beneath the rowan tree,
with your head on my chest you hummed to the sky?
Did it happen too fast? There was no talking to me.

Apple of my eye, come back one of these nights, soon,
and when my folks are out for the count we'll shoot the breeze;
I'll hold you in my arms beneath the halted moon,
hear your voice again say words like 'yes' and 'love' and 'please'.

Here the fire's still smouldering, its light is low,
and the key's under the doormat for you to find.
Ma and Da will be asleep; I'll be good to go;
hearts on our sleeves, we'll leave them all behind.

September

Night ushers in September
and streetlights flicker-flicker,

the last long evening leaves
but nobody grieves

when the last leaf quits its tree
to lay down autumn's decree

to not take with a pinch of salt
the clock's tick-tock default,

the river's insistence,
nor the forest's sense

of the ancientness of seasons,
the most ancient of treasons:

Eden, Adam and Eve,
of how there's no reprieve

from the evil
and the beautiful,

the sense of a time
before the word 'time',

before the word 'remember',
before the first September.

Time's Language

Time is a language:
summer's narrative begins in May's umbrage;

the notes of an old red wine
recount the terroir, the vine,

the weather, the harvest, the year;
the ripened blackberry bush says 'here,

taste your childhood, the fields
of your self', each bramble yields

a landscape on the verge
of forgetfulness, each mouthful a surge

of nose-breaths of cattle,
a five-bar gate's rattle,

each blade of grass a footfall,
each particle of soil part soul.

Spectator

A boy among a mass of men, the air
all Guinness and Powers in the stands, the ground
trampled burger boxes and plastic pint cups,
Ravenhill, the Ulster games, the sport
on the cusp of professionalism and money
and me on the cusp of boredom and manhood,
awkward teen ungrateful and uncommunicative.
Aeroplanes from the City Airport rose
behind the stand of seated season ticketers
as Otis and The Elevators
played 'Ghost Riders in the Sky' from the halfway line
and the team came out and I'd count down
the half on the War Memorial clock,
clap when everyone clapped, cheer at the cheers,
bemoan the referee on cue, pretended,
trying to be at least a semblance of a son.
To be a man like all those other men,
those other men, whom I picture now:
red faced, bustling for a place at the urinal,
filing out of the ground, full moon behind floodlights,
struggling to keep their boys close in the crush,
choosing the long roads back home to their lives.

Friendly

Windsor Park and I can see the shining white
of the German home kit under the floodlights,
the slender frame of Oliver Bierhoff,
his swarthy complexion, brown crop, the blond
of Klinsmann's mop, as he jogged the touchline
before unzipping his warm-up top, wheeking
off his trackies to come on in the second half,
his calves bulging the Adidas on his socks,
as home supporters cursed, bickered,
threw beer from the tier above

and then some fluky goalmouth scramble tap-in
of a goal for the hosts and suddenly
players hug, kiss, jump, pin each other down,
roll around together on the soaking turf,
steam rising from their passionate huddle

and then a momentary outbreak of touching
in the stands, a moment of each fan looking
the other in the eye, an instinctive grabbing,

and then the letting go, the looking away.

Flight

Behind the War Memorial Hall,
in the grounds of Tobar Muir Monastery,
in the middle of Crossgar yet hidden
by towering evergreens, down a tiny
pothole-ridden, unconcreted lane
where the alco-poppers and glue-sniffers gather,
is the home of the local football team,
corrugated iron covering the stand
where once as a kid I went with my Aunt
to watch my cousin play for Comber Seconds,
standing idly
            dreaming of Fiona from school,
the sway of the trees, what it would be like
to get out of this town and travel
to wherever those planes above were travelling,
the bigger leagues,
                as impossibly fast
and impossibly pumped
                a Mitre
struck me smack on the chops, and I bawled
on the touchline like a big child,
and wanted home.
                Story of my life.

Stadia

There's something industrial to stadia
and what are they, I guess, but extravagant sheds,
warehouses for the weekend warriors
with some grass in the middle, corrugated
containers, intent on being empty
mostly, because not every day can be match day
and not every match day a final, not every final
the last deciding day. We only need
a stadium for so long, as long
as the game's good.
                How quickly one decants
its fans at the death, pours them
into trains and taxis, seeps them
into bars and curry houses, drains them
back to their families, happier, angrier, both.

Prayer After Birth

for Felix

You've got it all in front of you, kiddo,
the fields along the Killyleagh Road
in blackberry September —
unlikeliest of the loveliest months —
the gentle stampede of cattle behind you,
stubbled ground beneath your feet; bird shadow.

You've got it all in front of you, kiddo,
a million miles an hour on your bike down the hill
to the pighouse and back up the lane again,
grazed knees and elbows, cuts and bruises,
gurning the house down, but you'll get it in time:
the readying, steadying, then the letting go.

You've got it all in front of you, kiddo,
kisses in the dark by the water at Whiterock,
between the night-time crickets at Quoile Lough,
before the last train at Waterloo,
beneath The New Globe by Mile End Canal;
kisses good luck, hello, goodbye, don't go.

You've got it all in front of you, kiddo,
the North Coast coastal road at August's end,
your grandfather burning bonfires in the spring,
and keep an eye out for a shooting star
above the ash tree in the winter,
and starlings, kiddo, from the kitchen window.

You've got it all in front of you, kiddo,
times tables and spellings and meanings,
kind-hearted people with bad breath reading stories
to you in a room with enormous windows

and a newly varnished parquet floor
where you'll begin to learn how much you'll never know.

You've got it all in front of you, kiddo,
snow fights and water bombs and sunburn,
cinema in the daytime with your mother
in the middle of the week, salted popcorn,
sweet popcorn, Coca-Cola, pick'n'mix,
thunder and lightning, silence, sunlight, rainbow.

You've got it all in front of you, kiddo,
stubbled ground beneath your feet; bird shadow,
the readying, steadying, then the letting go
of kisses good luck, hello, goodbye, don't go;
starlings, kiddo, from the kitchen window
where you'll begin to learn how much you'll never know

of thunder and lightning, silence, sunlight, rainbow.

Amen

in memory of Martha Ringland

On the morning of her funeral
when everyone had gathered in her house
to carry her coffin through Crossgar to church,
while the minister said the Lord's Prayer
and everyone bowed their heads in the living room,
I turned my back to look out to the garden
and saw a flutter of two robins land
on that unofficial classroom of my childhood.

. . . who art in heaven, hallowed be Thy name . . .

There's the coalbunker I filled the fire from
beside the space where I podded peas with her
hour after summer holiday hour.
And there's the space we laid the picnic blanket
which is also the space we brought the vinegar
to soothe the wasp sting on my little sister's leg.

. . . forgive us our trespasses, as we forgive those . . .

And at the bottom of that path she told me,
in short, that I should be a better brother
and not to give the others a hard time.
There's the shed we kept the croquet set
and there's the pigeonshit-spattered lawn we played on.

. . . lead us not into temptation, but deliver us . . .

And there, by the greenhouse, is the exact spot
from which she led my sister and myself
into the kitchen, gave us an ice cream
and told us how the butcher had been shot
by two masked men on motorbikes, in his shop.

. . . for Thine is the kingdom . . .

There's the fence I kicked the football over,
the bench we sat on in that photo in summer,
the space which used to be a pigeon coop
some of my grandfather's pigeons never returned to.

. . . the power and the glory . . .

And looking out through that window
that morning of neither sunlight nor rain
I fought back the tears and mustered one word.

Bolt

More north than you'd ever been, the Banffshire coast,
where fields are stripped in early April to their black-
earthed beginnings, charged with the promise
of harvest, where sea has found a way
to be by itself, washed up on shingle in forgotten
coves where light-bright gannets rule. This

was where we'd come to find a way to be
by ourselves, where it didn't rain the whole time, where
one day I glimpsed a deer two feet from me
on a coastal path, momentarily
snagged, twitching to break through a barbed-wire fence,
a frantic, electric panic, then freed, where
I thought how each of us is like that animal:
where the noise of its hooves as it bolted to the others
was heard as far as the ear could hear,
where it's bolting still, as far as the ear can hear.

A Stay in Spain

The dogs of Combarro are barking,
the owls are howling
and the forest is making its dawn noises.
The table's lamplight, the clock,
a blue that's becoming the morning's sky,
the trees casting off their silhouettes,
me scratching my sunburnt chest. There is truth
here, now. I catch my 6 a.m. reflection.
Shrieks from the woods; crickets; birds speaking.
Must every moment be stolen,
prised from the fingers of obligation,
appearance, profession, money?
Must we always wake earlier than each other
to get our heads straight? The morning moves so fast
and the harder you stare the brighter it gets. My skin
is chicken flesh; the window is open.
The walls are made of glistening stone,
glistening in the way beaches here glisten,
in the way thoughts glisten, and language,
the way silence can glisten, like now, like this.

Crossgar

You wouldn't have known the Monastery
is where the underage have congregated
to drink, for generations. There's no way
you could possibly have guessed the Post Office,
the tiny one which floods every winter,
has been sold off to the local petrol station-
cum-supermarket-cum-offy-cum-car showroom
as part of a national improvement scheme
for the *benefit* of the *community*.

It is understandably beyond you
to have predicted that the play park,
newly built — worth tens of thousands — could have been burnt
to cinders within a month of opening.
The Italians who own the pizzeria,
how could you have suspected
that they shut the shop each August, returning
home to their family in Napoli?

That woman walking down the street with the red nose,
who lives alone, and cannot read or write, 50 —
that her name is Joy, and she has a limp,
will have escaped you,

like the fact that here is where my grandfather
let me feed his racing pigeons, with dried corn
which they pecked from my tiny palm,
                                        this garden.

THE LOST POEMS OF GEORGES BERTRAND

Translations from his first collection Feu d'artifice

Refusing bitterness I walk with the river
once more and, once more, as if for the first
I see the multicoloured lights of the party boats,
hear their disjointed drunken jeering.
How alone is it possible to be
in a city where everyone loves one another,
in a city which loves itself, in a city
where love is *de rigueur, de mode*, the law.
You want the truth? Paris is a lie,
rotten with tradition, intransigent,
introspective, conservative to its back teeth.
What other country has a dress code,
frowns upon smiling, turns its nose up
if you don't speak the language, won't let you in?

⌣

It's not about love, Paris,
it's all about tradition;
everybody's in on
perpetuating its myths.

⌣

I'll never be bitter about my friends
and their successes. You have to believe
that every piece of literature —
a poem, a novel, a play — each book
in the end will get what it deserves
and no amount of nepotism, not even here
in the glassy, golden, red white and blue
tricolour-laden academies
with their jumped-up Johnny Come Latelies,

no amount of schmoozing with the big guns,
hotshots or the flash-in-the-pan populists
from the big Parisian publishing houses,
the university backslappers, none of this
can help you pull away the Golden Bough.

I'm remembering Café Métro, Oberkampf,
last summer, that arsey, snarky waiter
(who probably didn't help). She ordered
a noisette and a glass of water — typical.
'*Noisette* means hazelnut in English,' I said.
Of all the ways to break it off, she said,
there and then, 'I need to leave you, Georges.'
And that was that. I'm remembering that day,
how bright it was, so bright for early March.
How it had rained all those days before,
how it would rain for days to come.

You can't translate *terroir* to any other language.
It is the beating heart of French lexis.
I hear the word and I think of home.
There's something in the sound of the word itself
which mimics the undulations, elevations,
rolling quality of vineyards in the South.
It's almost as if in the beginning
the hills and soil and vines were thrown
upon the earth like a duvet upon a bed.
How much it's like the word terror; I'm reminded
of sneaking in, with Claude, to the neighbour's vineyard
and the rasping taste of stolen, out of season grapes.
Now I'm thinking of the night Claude died,

knocked down by a tractor during the harvest.
Terroir — terror. *Terroir* — *terre*. *Terroir* — tear.
Tear — to be torn. *Terroir, terre*, tier, tear.

〜

In my shitty apartment two floors above the launderette
across the road from the all-night light of the pharmacy
downstairs from the 24/7 dubstep party,
eleven stubbies of cheap Alsace stuff
the night before August's bank holiday.
I'd had enough, so I walked the path to the river
where I passed a down-and-out who said, and I'll never forget
the way he turned and looked me in the eye,
his both bloodshot, his tatty beard and his fingerless gloves,
how he grabbed my arm and said, 'You don't have to tell me,
    I know.'

〜

The truth is I don't mind the tourists mainly,
even the Americans, and their moccasins
and Ralph Lauren sweaters tied around their waists.
In fact I like their lack of pretension,
the effortlessness by which they remain themselves.
It's the Irish I have a problem with,
their smug presumption the world is in love with them,
their cloying accents, boozing and bad manners,
their cringeworthy attempts at jokes, at charm.
How can everything always be 'grand'?

〜

Every Saturday morning, before Café Bernard,
where I go for a coffee and the paper,

she's there at the desk twirling her hair
with one finger, bored, in front of a PC.
To say her hair is brown is the same as saying
the sea is blue, that the sky is blue.
When is the sea or the sky just blue?
So her hair, as she turns to face me, is brown
in the way that the sea is blue.
Her hair is never brown, in the way
that the sea is never blue. Blue is the word
given to the experience of the sea.
Brown, for the experience of her hair,
which is to say her hair is the sea, the sea her hair.

⌣

Melancholy is an empty classroom
ten minutes after the summer term's last bell,
ten minutes before the cleaners arrive,
ten minutes before I've packed my bag,
ten minutes after the students packed theirs.
I dare not count the classroom hours of my life,
nor the miles of corridors I've covered.
Perhaps there is no heaven, or hell
or even purgatory, perhaps there is a classroom
where someone talks us through the lives we've lived,
picks up on where we have gone wrong,
goes through mistakes, and corrections, says 'Now, repeat.'

⌣

The first evening of the summer holidays —
you've got to get it right. I walk home alone
in the early evening through the Jardin
du Luxembourg, past the popping tennis courts
and buy a bottle of cheap cold Champagne,

then grab a burger and *frites* from *Quick*
and meet some friends by the Seine.

～

And so it was by the Seine that I met Marie,
two years ago, at the end of the summer term.
She was a friend of a friend from university.
I walked her home and kissed her at the door
and on the stairs and in the bedroom
and even after swallowing that pill —
the morning after — she held my hand
and she kissed me then, she even kissed me then.

～

I've already had a month away
from work, to find my thoughts returning
to just that, work. I think of explorers
who've struck out on their own, the hardest paths,
setbacks, and naysayers ignored.
To be like that, to shun security,
to roll the dice on yourself, what you might be,
to leave the bitchiness and gossip
of this 9-5 cesspool, its men and women
with talents for nothing but admin —
who wants praise for fastidiousness? —
where it pays to do what you're told, say yes,
where mortgages and pensions are god.
Who is remembered for his efficiency
or paying off his mortgage, collecting his pension?
So what is it that stops me, what fence
between the grass on the other side and here?

～

Taking a southbound train from Paris-Gare de Lyon
for a stint at home reminds me of that passage
from *Howards End*, that bit about
train stations, signifying something
like infinity, the high steel structures.
'There is something else,' they're telling us,
beyond this bubble of bistros and brothels
and fat cats and layabouts and soaks and workaholics.
And they're saying, 'you have forgotten yourself.'
I search for my reflection in the carriage window
but it's too bright, too early for that.

Three summers ago my father disappeared,
not in the middle of the night
but mid-morning, we reckon,
not returning home for lunch, which was bizarre.
All I can ever picture is the half carafe
of Côte du Rhone, the Reblochon,
the whole tomato, sliced, and of course
the half baguette, unbroken, the clock
advancing, my mother beginning
to shoo the flies away.

And I can picture his clothes
hanging in his wardrobe —
which none of us can bear to face —
thick cotton button-downs, ironed,
the silk ties, linen trousers,
his good leather shoes all lined up,
Chelsea boots, penny loafers, brogues,

some left to loosen with shoes trees,
polished black, and left shining in the dark.

⸻

Every day is a day the disappeared
do not return, but you can't live on hope.
This evening it's balmy, the window
of my old bedroom here in my old home
is open. After this I will walk somewhere,
somewhere there is a view of all of this,
remember where I'm from and maybe
if I'm lucky who I am, but after this.
And maybe there will be sky like sky
from my youth, and light like that light
at the top of the hill I think of
in the city when I just need to think.
All those lost things coming back. After this.

Becoming a Box Set Detective

I've often wondered if I'd make the grade
as a box set detective, you know the ones:
functioning alcoholics who wear the same jacket,
don't wash their hair, polish their shoes, have trouble
fitting in, difficulty remembering
to eat, or simply not eating at all,
unashamedly parading their regional accent.
The consonants of their foreign language
crash like a precious vase in an empty
candle-lit country house near a forest;
like the bricked-in window of a seaside cottage;
like a jackknifed backup car at a crossroads.
They have a past, a secret, a darkness
in their soul, a loved one they don't want
to talk about, even in the pub
where they either leave too early or stay too late.
Their history will not stop tailing them,
even in their final season, especially then.
I've wondered if I could join the ranks
of those self-centred ones, forgetting family birthdays,
suspended for not filing paperwork,
not giving *a shit about the goddam paperwork.*
They struggle with orders and authority figures,
the ones who drive through cities, over bridges,
looking moody to ambient music,
puzzling over a clue, a body, a message,
in dependable Classic cars,
who force open their door to heaps of post,
bills they're either too cool or depressed to pay,
who always stand, at night, before the mirror
accosted by some god-awful flashback
before sink-splashing their dog-tired faces
and sighing. They wake never having slept,
in a chair, with the curtains undrawn,
case papers and photos strewn about them;

they pinch the bridge of their nose and wince,
then a phone rings, but they never say *hello*
or *what?*, answering always with their name:
Morse, Berthaud, Wallander, Luther, Saga.
I want, like them, to confront the criminal —
after a long chase scene at a great height
on a precarious ledge — who always brags
we're not so different, you and I, Inspector,
the culprit you always fail to guess,
the misguided crazy-eyed zealot
on some seemingly crazy-assed mission,
masquerading as a 9-5 man
such as, say, an English teacher
who wanted to set the world on fire with words.
I want to be able to reason: *The game's over, buddy,*
how did you really think this would end?

The International Balloon Fiesta

The International Balloon Fiesta
has been on my mind — hot air hobbyists
in their hundreds, firing themselves skyward.
What for? Who are they trying to impress
at the International Balloon Fiesta?
This airborne pageant, this peculiar parade
of past-timers, this throwback to patchwork,
to basket, balloon and wind direction,
this Blytonesque thrill of boyish buoyancy,
this bird-like dependence on thermal rise and fall.
The International Balloon Fiesta
has still been on my mind, despite the news
of its postponement due to bad weather,
despite the news of the mess in the Middle East
and the shootings of a psycho in the States.
Despite the news someone has organized
an International Balloon Fiesta
and invited the world and his wife.
At the end of days please let there be
an International Balloon Fiesta,
one last hurrah before it goes tits up,
a rise in the face of the rising sea.

Anti-acknowledgements

I wouldn't like to acknowledge the nobs downstairs
who, despite the many times I've counted to ten
and asked, without expletives, won't turn the bass down.

I am in no way indebted to them
and their Hendrix and Led Zep phases,
respectively. The time they lit a fire
at 4 a.m. in the backyard has added
nothing to my endeavours. I couldn't
be less grateful to them.

                 My landlord, non-pareil,
deserves no credit whatsoever
for never fitting draft excluders
onto the front door or into the windows,
taking weeks to unblock the sink
and replace the filament in the fan oven.
If it wasn't for his wonderful
negligence so much more of this would have been possible.
He's truly made my life more complicated.

To all my friends who've never bought my book:
words can't convey my scorn.
                     This is for them.

Northern Ireland is a constant source
of homesickness and identity crisis
without which I could imagine a happier life.
Particular thanks to my teachers, and
the village of Crossgar.

X: thanks for the sleepless nights and writer's block;
anytime I go to Portheras Cove
or drive down those corridory Cornish roads
in the unreal light of a vintage summer,

get lost on a walk, or in somebody else's eyes
across a table outside a Parisian café,
eat scones encased in clotted cream
and (my favourite) raspberry jam,
anytime I taste spice in a Shiraz,
or get a tannin tongue from too much tea
I'll think of you.

All the Pretty Horses

Tonight I'm saddling up with John Grady
on a grey white horse he's broken in
but doesn't want to lose. For dinner we've eaten
beans and tortilla and cheese outside and kicked
the campfire down to ashes and — good God —
the stars. I'm trying not to talk
unnecessarily. Tonight it's warm
and the moon bright enough, says John,
to guide our way. 'Mexico tomorrow'
are the only words he utters for an hour,
what feels like an hour. Night air, horse hooves
drumming the bone-dry ground; you feel
the leather reins between your palms. He leads,
and that's all right, sometimes muttering
to his animal. It feels good to be galloping
south, the sky lightening with each mile.
We stop at an arroyo near the border,
water the horses, breakfast on buttermilk biscuits
he takes wrapped in gingham from his satchel,
share sweetened coffee from his tin cup
before we ask each other questions
about what we have, about what we want
in this life, work, love, crossing the border.

The Grapes of Wrath

This Sunday afternoon I'm picking peaches
in a Californian orchard with Tom Joad.
An orchard full of peaches in the summer
on the west coast, where every colour
is the colour of summer, and it's hard to believe
these are hard times — we keep only the perfect fruit
and leave the rest to rot. But I've watched
the way he scoffs the fallen stuff, stashes it
about himself, his bony, sallow self —
too young to be rubbing the small of his back like that —
the desperate way he barters at the drugstore.
The sun beats and our buckets aren't even
half empty. I'd give him some of mine,
all of mine, but this afternoon, the 1930s,
there isn't enough of anything.
                                    Why can't
I get away from here, the hungry anger
of his eyes, flies circling bruised flesh in the dust?
.

Joy Division at The Haçienda

This afternoon, it's tonight, The Haçienda,
four pale-faced twenty-somethings, plugging in,
exchanging glances and nods, a 1-2-3,
playing songs with titles like 'Disorder',
its lyrics like a broken record, 'feeling, feeling, feeling'.
I'm one of the first to hear those opening notes,
watch that convulsive front man
who seems to be on drugs
or in need of drugs or a hot meal
as he stares out beyond the crowd,
the walls, to the north,
the city, to all the norths, and all their cities
and all the lights of all the houses
of all the men who having eaten want more,
or maybe it's to the audience of himself,
the north of himself, his soul's streets, and houses
lit through a winter fog, closing in.

Pet Sounds

It's just gone midnight, but the sun is beating
down on the sidewalk, on the beaches,
the palm trees, the wet blond hair of surfer dudes,
kissing the salt-water shoulders of surfer girls,
glaring off the polished chrome on Cadillacs
and Chevies and primary colour camper vans.
I'm walking down the corridor of a high-rise,
lined with silver and gold and platinum discs.
At Capitol Records Brian Wilson
is in the studio at the piano
with Tony Asher, in loud shirts, arguing
only sometimes about the arrangements,
the music with words, the words with music,
'I keep trying, I keep trying to find,
I keep trying to find a place to fit in,
I keep trying', as outside time moves on,
night happens, and day leaves them behind
at black and white keys, a chorus of stars.

County Almost

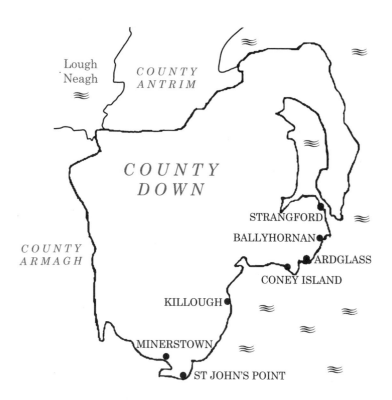

Lough
Neagh

*COUNTY
ANTRIM*

*COUNTY
DOWN*

*COUNTY
ARMAGH*

STRANGFORD

BALLYHORNAN

ARDGLASS

CONEY ISLAND

KILLOUGH

MINERSTOWN

ST JOHN'S POINT

I MINERSTOWN

At Minerstown I could have cried, mountains,
seaweed, the sun, trying, a black dog
swimming with its topless owners
in July's cold currents, the promise of seals.
Narrow concrete steps take you down
to a feeling that smacks of childhood.
What is it? What is it about a place
like this, like Minerstown, the old man
perched on his sea-facing front step, drinking a cup
like a lost character from a Steinbeck novel,
that churns me up like a chump,
a back-home-for-the-holiday hire-car driver
who shouldn't find these roads so hard to navigate,
the views so hard to name,
the history so hard to explain.

2 ST JOHN'S POINT

A kind of Nowhereville-on-Sea, striped black and yellow
the lighthouse is locked up to the public —
unmanned as now controlled remotely —
and I can't recall coming here as a kid
to this white-walled bastion of abandon,
the kind of place for an indie album photo shoot,
wild water, ugly rocks, elements unpreened,
on the edge of things, and almost beautiful,
almost unfamiliar, a kind of County Almost
where we parked, walked around, and watched
the fishermen on a boat, out in the deep,
standing shakily with their lines,
before driving back down the windy roads
which brought us here, chased by swifts,
surveilled by big birds balancing on telegraph wires,
until the manor with impossible flowers.

3 KILLOUGH

Not quite the back of beyond, there's something
about Killough, the tree-lined thoroughfare,
newly painted window frames. A man cross-legged
on a wall having a smoke on his own
opposite the pub where I took a wrong turn
which led us to a dead-end by the sea.
Conversations from car doors, street-side fuel pumps,
the three pubs, one of which promises
music at the weekend. The four wee girls
waiting to cross the road with a massive speaker,
singing and dancing to an American voice,
channelling Beyoncé or Gaga
and all the other independent women
as you give me directions, and I take them.

4 CONEY ISLAND

The sky darkened at Coney Island
as a family unpacked on the beach
guarded by a stud-collared Great Dane;
a man swam. Down a tiny ill-signed turn-off
it's like a beach that doesn't want to be a beach
and with its weeds and stones almost isn't.
Past the holiday lets and down the potholed lane,
slipping on seaweed, wondering
if this was the way, feeling like intruders, alone.
We stopped, agreed 'this must be it',
looked out to sea, talked of where we'd come from,
parents, family, the future, held each other,
then back to the car before the rain,
and the tide, and it got too late, before
I started to talk of my failings, grasp
the edge of my talent at the edge of the sea.

5 ARDGLASS

I used to work in a care home here, Ardview,
mashing up boiled eggs and margarine
in ramekins so they could spread it on their toast,
endless stainless steel teapots, cups and saucers
used washed dried, used washed dried, disposable
pots of jam, and marmalade.
Doing the rounds in the afternoon
with a coffee urn and a tub of Family Circle,
louder each time, 'Would you like a wee drink of tea?',
disinfectant and 'Caution Wet Floor' signs
in the corridors, news of someone
who made it as far as the bus stop last night.
The bedroom that wasn't vacant last week;
the TV room's panorama of the Irish Sea;
photographs of grandchildren; hard sweets;
whodunnits, murder mysteries on the shelves;
the dog-eared *Connect 4, Cluedo, Scrabble*;
somebody forgetting a name, all jumbled up.

6 ARDGLASS MARINA

The bins at the Marina overflowed
during the Twelfth fortnight, as three lads
in Gaelic tracksuits chewed gum, shot the breeze
going down the street to where Cochrane's
ice-cream shop is now called something else
but on the whole it feels as if someone's hit 'pause'
round here; even the fisheries are dead.
But the glassy high-rise apartments
bear testament to our age-old demand
for a property by water, how much we'll pay
for what: scope, a lookout, a sense of elevation,
summer G and Ts on the balcony,
a share in the ocean's profundity?
The seagulls pick at flotsam in the car park.
I point out where an old friend used to live
who told me Ardglass means Green Heights.
The heavens open, so we drive away and leave
all the little tycoons to sell the sea.

7 BALLYHORNAN BEACH

Rain holds off, roads narrow past St Patrick's Well
at which we don't feel like the detour,
carry on instead to a beach behind council houses.
Down the steps and out along the shore
teetering by the tide in unsuitable shoes
a day away from being back in Bristol.
For a minute I imagine never leaving
and don't tell you. A tractor rumbles on,
the mobile butcher does the rounds.
I imagine staying, as a father wades in
with his son. I imagine not going back
even now I am back, and it's sunny
and everyone's going to the zoo with their kids
and the train's arrival is buffered by trees,
the mixed fig plant is outgrowing its pot.
If I wanted I could play 'Jackie Wilson Said'
on vinyl and eat all the cherries in the fridge.

8 STRANGFORD

We'd only meant to stop at Minerstown
in the morning and then head back for lunch.
To show you something of the sea round here,
to kill some time before our flight that night.
But the road had other ideas for us
and it became the afternoon, Strangford,
an 'artisan' café we had to ourselves,
the quiet of a midweek town at half-past-three
in the middle of an overcast July.
The edge of a county on the edge
of Europe. We reached the bottom
of our coffees and took to the wheel again,
going home to pack, to leave, to go home.
The Quoile, Portulla Wood and Finnebrogue.
Weeks later all I think of is coastal road,
all a self is, all a county is, where they end.

Acknowledgements

Grateful acknowledgement is due to the editors of the following publications where some of these poems, or versions of them, were published first: *The Irish Times, Modern Poetry in Translation, Poem, The Moth, Poetry Ireland Review* and *Poetry London.*

Thanks are due to the Newcastle Centre of Literary Arts for asking me to participate in their 'Poetics of the Archive' project, from which came 'Anti-acknowledgements' and 'The Lost Poems of Georges Bertrand'.

I am grateful to the Centre Culturel Irlandais for a Residential Language Bursary during the summer of 2014 which helped me to write 'Souvenir'.